YOU CAME TO MEET SOMEONE ELSE

BY THE SAME AUTHOR:

STEPPING OUT—UNICORN PRESS
IN THE RED MEADOW—NEW RIVERS PRESS
DYING TO SURVIVE—DOUBLEDAY & CO.
LIGHTER-THAN-NIGHT VERSE—RED HILL PRESS
SWIFTLY NOW—UNIVERSITY OF OHIO PRESS
A SPOOL OF BLUE, New and Selected Poems—SCARECROW PRESS

YOU CAME TO MEET SOMEONE ELSE

Poems by

CAROLYN STOLOFF

Santa Maria • Asylum Arts
1993

ACKNOWLEDGEMENTS

The author wishes to express thanks to the editors of the following publications, in which some of these poems first appeared: *The Agni Review*, "Bad Day"; *Alcatraz*, "In the Half Light", "Inscription on a Stele Circa 1950", "The Professor"; *Art Times*, "Reflection"; *Asylum Annual*, "Leaving a Head Behind"; *Blue Buildings*, "At My Bidding" (as "Behind Spring's Raised Fingers"); *Caliban*, "When the Sky Smells of Burning Sapphires"; *Caprice*, "Disturbance in a Family"; *Chaminade Literary Review*, "From the Souk in Marrakesh", "From the Barrens"; *Chelsea*, "Facts", "For Your Information"; *The Connecticut Poetry Review*, "Door to the Closet" (as "There's a Hidden Door to the Closet"); *Contact II*, "Correction for Astigmatism", "The Sneeze", "Working at Knots", "Liquor at Five" (as "Going Places"); *The Hudson River Anthology*, "In the Game Find The Dog"; *Images*, "The Dusty Ones"; *Pearl*, "Defender of the Faith"; *Pembroke Magazine*, "Ascending the Cape Memling's Madonna Wears", "In the Miraculous Chapel"; *Poetry Motel*, "About Straight Chair", "Turning Out"; *Poets On:*, "Dialogue", "Delegation"; *The Signal*, "It's in the Cards", "O Powerful", "What Can Be the Use of Them", "Manipulator"; *The Southern Poetry Review*, "Moon"; *Thunder Mountain Review*, "The Painter of Skyscapes".

"A Built Bridge, Footnotes" was included in the Light Years' anthology *Sometime The Cow Kick Your Head*.

The following poems first appeared in *Lighter-Than-Night Verse*, published by Red Hill Press: "Illumination", "Who's Tired", "Be a Maverick", "The Ritz", "Everyone Knows What Hartmann is About", "Birds Eye", "The Difficult Countries".

Copyright © 1993 by Carolyn Stoloff

ISBN 1-878580-38-8
Library of Congress Catalogue Number: 93-70301

Printed in the United States of America.

Cover painting, Giorgio de Chirico, *Two Masks*
© Estate of Giorgio de Chirico / VAGA, New York 1993
Photo courtesy of Scala/Art Resource, New York

Asylum Arts
P. O. Box 6203
Santa Maria, CA 93456

CONTENTS

I

DOOR TO THE CLOSET	11
IN DRY DOCK	12
WHEN THE SKY SMELLS OF BURNING SAPPHIRES	13
DISTURBANCE IN A FAMILY	15
AFTER BREAKFAST	17
IN THE CENTRAL STATION	18
LEAVING A HEAD BEHIND	20
ROMANCE	22
O POWERFUL!	24
CHRISTMAS IS NOT OBSERVED BY TURKEYS	25
LIQUOR AT FIVE	26
THE DELEGATION	27
THE DUSTY ONES	28
DEAD RECKONING	29

II

REFLECTION	33
RIDDLE	34
THE SCHEME	35
TURNING OUT	36
CORRECTION FOR ASTIGMATISM	37
A BUILT BRIDGE, FOOTNOTES	38
ABOUT STRAIGHT CHAIR	39
FROM VENCE, FRANCE	40
CHANGING FOCUS	41
ILLUMINATION	42
FOR YOUR INFORMATION	44
WHO'S TIRED	46
BE A MAVERICK	48
THE RITZ	49
EVERYONE KNOWS WHAT HARTMANN IS ABOUT	50
BIRDS EYE	51
THE DIFFICULT COUNTRIES	52

III

A SOMEONE AS GOOD AS ANY	55
IN THE SWIM	57
HOME	59

INSCRIPTION FOUND ON A STELE CIRCA 1950	61
IN THE HALF LIGHT	63
FACTS	65
FROM THE BARRENS	67
THE SNEEZE, Notes for an Essay	68
WHAT CAN BE THE USE OF THEM	70
BAD DAY	72
THE PROFESSOR	73

IV

ASCENDING THE CAPE MEMLING'S MADONNA WEARS	77
IN THE GAME FIND THE DOG	79
IT'S IN THE CARDS	81
THE PAINTER OF SKYSCAPES	83
MANIPULATOR	85
MOON	86
THE OPTIMIST	87
DEFENDER OF THE FAITH	88
IN THE MIRACULOUS CHAPEL	89
BEHIND SPRING'S RAISED FINGERS	90
WORKING AT KNOTS	91
DIALOGUE	92
FROM THE SOUK IN MARRAKESH	93

You Came to Meet Someone Else

For Robert Peters

DOOR TO THE CLOSET

when you reach for the corduroy jacket
a coat tumbles down
like a cousin from a train
that hasn't quite stopped

you came to meet someone else
but you offer him a hand
he takes your mouth

your knees buckle
his suitcase moans
it's just like the last time
the mouths don't fit
they are both yours

he takes your hand and tosses it
to a field behind the station
you sprint to catch it
it's a green apple
you sink your teeth in
it tastes warm and salty

you pitch the apple into a bush
it lands in an open suitcase
filled with hearts
they pulse like infant mice
around the apple

hands clap over your eyes
a perfect fit
you feel behind you
is that you Jack?
but your hands meet
each other

IN DRY DOCK

nurse tapes a plastic vein to his arm
she presses firm fingers on his wrist
nurse — a chest of buttons and glass rods —
smoothes the sheet over the sailor

he would like to crack the unhatching egg
of her belly, her hard-boiled cheeriness,
her pale porous skin
nurse is not a sea, not a deliverance

carnations pass the frame of the open door
followed by starched paper boats
water would soften
sometimes flexible young nurses flash

the sailor would like
to release them in the East River
just over the sill   he would like to lean
and watch them float out of sight
of the hospital schedule and finding himself up
leap into the waterway
to swim after them for dear life

the sailor smacks
the bedpost with his foot   he wants
to shift his stone freight
he smiles weakly at the crane
hovering over him . . . would she . . . please . . .
he would like to turn   he would like

to lift nurse from her efficient feet
and hurl her off the dock, to turn his back
as narwhales zero in, and her shrieks
gleam like flying fish

WHEN THE SKY SMELLS OF BURNING SAPPHIRES

swelling with cobalt fire, the sky
runs to great lengths   it defoliates
telegraph poles   decaying replies
fall from their nests

it's not icons we need
the women wear pensive cheeks and gold
of a single hue   an icon Child
is muzzled with sorrow

let Him mouth his toys
let Him squirm on her lapis lap and wail
a fortuitous solo
a fresh gust that jiggles the halos,

pierces our veils
flips the score so high songs of violins
can sail safe over tongues of antennae
over bricks rinds and beggars' sores

when the sky smells of blue bays
a bulb sprouts in a violin's belly
a yellow lily promising play
strains toward an onyx moon a milky moon

have you grown forelegs for the wind's
vanguard?   have you a quest?
a question that quarrels?

when the sky smells of burning sapphires
it's not an icon I want
I must dance for the dead whose toes
point up and out in the diction of motion

down the Street of Gold there's a bow
that can fiddle a channel through an icefloe,
a grey man's chest, a flute note
that can lasso a missile

it's not an icon I want
I must squirm on Earth's lap
I must wail for the quick — now, because now
the sky's burning

DISTURBANCE IN A FAMILY

for an anxious father combing his daughter's eyes
there's a shrine with no door
he stores his moustache in his navel at bedtime
a nail longs to be interred

there's a shrine with no door
it's a lie of separation
a nail longs to be interred
he stands on splintered boards calling across water

it's a lie of separation
a foot doesn't walk alone
he stands on splintered boards calling across water
tide's foaming edge advances

a foot doesn't walk alone
where wind fills prints with sand
tide's foaming edge advances
mother runs back and forth on the littoral

where wind fills prints with sand
clutching a bundle of gypsy cloth
mother runs back and forth on the littoral
composing an opera in a foreign tongue

clutching a bundle of gypsy cloth
caught in flight, a lover looks down at the ocean
composing an opera in a foreign tongue
who has not reached for the brass ring?

caught in flight, a lover looks down at the ocean
where monks in blue rise from graves
who has not reached for the brass ring?
no sin is original

where monks in blue rise from graves
she measures her nails daily
no sin is original
grenades sleep in the undergrowth

she measures her nails daily
he retrieves his moustache from his navel at sunrise
grenades sleep in the undergrowth
for an anxious daughter combing her father's eyes

AFTER BREAKFAST

Ossabaw Island, Georgia

a wet snout presses against a pane
she tugs at the door
for breakfast they drank silence
now the man runs barefoot on the shore

she tugs at the door
surf compulsively scrubs sand
a man runs barefoot along the shore
recalling her cheek against his hand

surf compusively scrubs sand
oriflammes flare from the horizon
the thought of his hand on her skin
sends her warmth flowing across the pasture

oriflammes herald dawn
behind him palmettos splay green swords
her heart pours across the pasture
to where the beekeeper whispers to his bees

behind him, the palmettos' raised swords
a mouse floats belly up in the fountain
the beekeeper whispers to his bees
about night-deaths accomplished

a mouse floats belly up
the car must be near water
day's deaths are accomplished
where squeals rend the morning air

the car must be near the bay
they drank silence for breakfast
as squeals from the barnyard fade away
a wet snout nuzzles her palm

IN THE CENTRAL STATION

love's last local departs from track 26
sand slips past his waist
he puts his bifocals in the case
hoping her lamp will lead him home

as sand slips past his waist
he imagines lunging into the thicket of her hair
hoping her lamp will lead him home
before he trips on his horizon

he imagines lunging into the thicket of her hair
as a tool extends an arm
before he trips on his horizon
there are no props for the next scene

as a tool extends an arm
his call must swing back June's gate
there are no props for the next scene
when a man lashed to his core yearns for the sirens

his call must swing back June's gate
even in winter
when a man lashed to his core yearns for the sirens
and the body gives up its orchestra

even in winter
when frost flings white gloves on the earth
and the body gives up its orchestra

a man must clutch the pole and pull himself
                    onto the moving platform

when frost flings white gloves on the land
he puts his bifocals in the case
a man must clutch the pole and pull himself
                    onto the moving platform
love's last local leaves from track 26

LEAVING A HEAD BEHIND

the housewife hangs her head
on a hook inside the broom closet door
and rushes heedless into the lettuce
tearing and drenching

she will begin again . . .
she begins again among branches
of the oldest tree in Virginia
below her, fans huddle waving with used hankies
to cheer is easy, she thinks
it's the trust, the living trust, she's after
not those laundry bags stuffed with apologies

laddering her tights in the descent
she puts her foot down on the flag
in a field crows have deserted
where padded men marked with numbers
once collided and passed the pig

here, carefully, she will raise balloons
and cut their stems to release them
here she will nurture potatoes
fertilized with remorseless official forms
and the root strength money can buy

she festoons the fence with lilacs and
light hearts snapping her fingers at
authorities in her bones —

brittle elders offering the option
of dignified collapse

meanwhile an ant kingdom's fingers
climb the cabinet to the sink
and her closeted head, having no body
but its own to blame, dissolves
in the reign of darkness

ROMANCE

on the range a heart stew simmers
raven blinks down from a beam
sea wind stirs in the box beneath her bed of clover
lifting her tresses, he presses moist lips to her nape

the raven opens its bill but says nothing
always I've wanted always she confides
opening her hair he presses moist lips to her nape
behind mist a gale sweeps a field for the dancers

always I've wanted always she confesses
why does the wind cease at sundown?
behind mist a gale sweeps a field for waltzing
come to Mandalay and bring your dreams he sings

why does wind die at sundown?
do fishes fly where you live? she asks him
come to Mandalay and see he whispers
soiled veils blow away one by one

do fishes play where you live? she questions
earth like an infant head burrows and comes 'round
soiled veils blow away one by one
he says *even a small sail enlivens the horizon*

earth shaped like an infant head burrows and comes 'round
lost hunger, has it begun again?
he says *even a distant sail enlivens the horizon*
a spring uncoils in her broken hand

lost hunger . . . it begins again
he calls *come look at the moon's path! let's follow it*
spring unfurls in her broken hand
she or the rock trembles

he calls *come look at the moon's path on water*
sea wind stirs beneath her bed of clover
she or the coast trembles
the stew of hearts boils over

O POWERFUL!

nothing can replace the veneer of purpose
on the fifth pilgrim's foot
and despoil the petty officer of his pettiness
nothing can rob the swamp of its moisture

what can deflate our carnival rodomontade?
what can reduce its noisy bluster
to deaf space?
what can put a stop to irrational numbers
as they boil over recording hairs
on the toes of bacteria?
yes yes nothing

nothing can replace the veneer of purpose
on the fifth pilgrim's foot with a
galloping crystal star, a rooted river, yes
nothing — disguised in spiritual fur
and tattooed with Egyptian vowels
I sing of thee o powerful
O hungry Nothing

it's indecent
what's indecent?
Nothing — used chiefly as a solvent
for an infinity of one . . . to numb
eyeballs and the tongue

this Nothing has been nagging the petty officer
nagging nagging nagging
our petty officer since dawn

CHRISTMAS IS NOT OBSERVED BY TURKEYS

the flock held its breath as rich loads shot up
    and were capped
during the drilling no one said "ouch"
everyone looked good   well-oiled

federally insured delays guaranteed
    oversight as examiners looked over
    and above rising debts through what airspace
    was left   into the distance

piles of tacitness passed from hand to hand
(underhand actually   and with both hands)
and rolling loans filled vacancies at the table
    in time to say "I pass" with gross abandon
    when questioned

as for regularly tapped sources papered over . . .
there was time to clean soil from under the nails

caught in the mystique of self-expansion
each followed his star
to the stable   commitment was the bottom line
while it paid off

the boom would last for. . . .
well, to forget is divine

LIQUOR AT FIVE

in the morning we fight for our plots
pile on layers
until our towers shudder

after noon we confer
stuff boxes with papers, fold linens
work jaws and fingers
until joints crack like old cups

we share liquor at five
it rockets us into a clockless skyscape
in sample homes — Leo, Cancer —

we float above bleached sheets
clandestine encounters
cruise without contracts
brush off life's stains

wayfarers through day, our sanctuary
is the place breath goes at dusk —
the whiteness left

when pigment runs off a landscape
into light's still
there, no one can build
on less than harmony

THE DELEGATION

we left gifts
they were taken at night

a week passed   at last
natives stepped from thickets
into the sun

moistening our lips
we offered them communion —
red beads, pots. . . .

a flashlight finished them

the headman's spine
cracked with fear
when the light blared

we bartered
even our rifles

museums snapped up
the spirit ships
we did well

everyone loves a hunt
when it's come as you like
and take all

the next time, we
were taken

THE DUSTY ONES

on the journey toward rain
past crumbling cisterns, past grain
sprung up where nomads flung seeds,
they raise tents at dusk
on walls that once checked them
walls sanded to stumps by wind

under a tangle of high-pitched
chatter, men unstrap carpets, dates,
goatskins fat with water

when soldiers bolt city gates,
when only an unpacked camel
can squeeze, head down,
through the narrow slot
and merchants follow on foot

nomads turn out pockets
for the last prophet's crumbs
in the temple of space
and of the heart — an ancient site
where love collects like water

at night a little flame
alters the solitude   men crouch
in its ark, a tribal core,
parting each other's beards,
thick as walls,
for a glimpse of God's mouth

DEAD RECKONING

nimble at shinnying
knotting lines coiled in the sun
or stretched,

each seaman rode his crests
knew his calms
each sought his Punt Cherbourg
Mars in the spyglass

squalls overlapped
together men watched the moon,

heard creaks, slops,
great groans as she rolled,

the rasp as boys swayed
in salt-stiffened shrouds
calling singing

from the yards gulls peered down
as we took on speed

shipboard chores busy us
engines hum
still we remain

at sea —

gulls circle as we
steam toward a point
to load or unload
depending on orders

about our orders . . .

a captain paces
diviner of lodestones
reef-prophet by grace of charts,

keeper of astrolabe, sextant,
at last chronometers built in

to birds somehow   birds —

born with instruments
tuned to fixed ports

needing more we're moved
one place to another
further,

an outmost shore

REFLECTION

what a gorgeous lie! —
"moonlight"   I wake reflecting
how each eye's a port-
hole in night's hull,

snip of the hologram
holding it whole   note
how neatly moon fits
a pupil, its parent

but what's apparent
isn't   sun's responsible
for the old man's glow

but no, just now
it was I who lit the bright
disc in you, English and full

RIDDLE

it's huge   yet a man
walking his acre
can shield it with a penny

●

though it covers the meadow by day
it's nothing like a rug

●

or a hat
though it rests on our heads

●

without chart or compass it sails
in a direction neither left
nor righteous

●

it glows like a peeled papaya

but it's more like an apricot
on a small tree — our galaxy —
at the edge of a Sahara

THE SCHEME

the germ of a scheme sinks
it develops a nose — its host's nose
it speaks through its nose
and wagers against waves

born with a taste for hearts
and a stalking skill, the scheme
begins to purr, to spend
to become a smooth citizen

held in common like a handshake
it collects mansions
and connections
with noses in all directions

look! a temple! and our scheme
in the tabernacle

TURNING OUT

Public Sentiments buckle up
check their guns
march in neat rows
to the heart's tattoo
across the white square of my page

hurt, spotted with mud —
after miles on foot —
what's private hangs back

can't train a plum's spurt
love's flush
the clutch of fear in the veins

can't salute shame

but the Private wants fame
to be cast
monumental in bronze   to parade
naked in uniform

CORRECTION FOR ASTIGMATISM

you can't stop short of it
a chasm three feet deep
sticks to your toes
you're acrophobic
you can't take a step

if you do
the earth, an aroused crocodile
comes up to meet you

but it's there again — the drop
you can't pick it off
hit the dust to be done with it
oops! it hangs from your chin

if you take off your glasses
the chasm leaps into your arms
the crocodile slides through your lips
all your feet retreat
as after a last curtain call
the dust claps

and rises to leave

A BUILT BRIDGE, FOOTNOTES

a bridge all-at-once-
without-future has no head
and future is a head depend on it
a face with eyes facing ahead
and a nose

a bridge doesn't have a nose

it doesn't know which way to go
to go forward
so it doesn't   it stays

though if you abridge you certainly get
to the other end faster
even walking backward
than if you descend into the canyon
shortsighted and scholarly
counting pinecones

all spine, bridge may collapse
vertebra by vertebra
into the gorge or river   or dangle
depending

until then it maintains a rigid ambivalence

a boat is different

ABOUT STRAIGHT CHAIR

straight chair's armless yes
but not defeated

not clothed, it wears
itself cheerfully

as would you, were you chair

a legless man's a
legless man

a chair, without legs,
isn't one

no chairs kneel

some chairs face walls:
shamed chairs

tight-kneed restless men
can't stand sitting

address the chair please!

up front, pregnant with poise,
chair expects

crowds cheer power's seat
time backs up to it

vote chair

FROM VENCE, FRANCE

when night empties the mountain's height
I ask with the blind : *what* valley?

light liberates rocks from touch,
vision from dreams, feet from clay

or how can we know how high we've come?

cypresses plug earth in sky
a waterfall is the sky's necktie

at a lizard's end, his stump
gropes for its tail again

one hand roots, or holds off sleep
two hands shape loaves, fresh daily

CHANGING FOCUS

Manhattan

May slaps her tuning fork
on this spit of land   green notes
spring open   earth hums

prudent police tilt their badges
flashing light around corners
clean cool co-eds spread like chickweed
on the park's astonished bed

watch the chauffeur extract
his stiff widow from her Cadillac
resilient as a cockatoo,
she crosses the rain-washed pavement
in front of Saks

in cement canyons, brokers corral
stocks under a polluted sky
horns clash
in their pools, nubile typists chatter
above clattering keys

review with me winter's crises:
toppling tower-men,
well-groomed hands waving wildly
above quicksand. . . .

let's focus on all that's gone awry —
now . . . shift your eyes
to that butterfly

ILLUMINATION

> "Eyes need more help than mouth
> because mouth is always moving."
> — Pablo of Elizabeth Arden

Because light changes
the light you'll be seen in —
morning, office, at-home light
the way someone who loves you
looks by your lamp

Because daylight's the most difficult
a woman is likely to be seen by
(precisely, unjustly, like the mirror's lie)
and is not the light in places
a woman looks to look nice
to see her real face
the face exposed by the night

Because light itself
(men in general) is harsh
and office light knows no justice
women like evening light
the light that makes the average male
look close, look nourishing
look like someone who might
see one as loveable, makes him appear
to be someone who loves *you* for instance
the setting to make up in
to make love by
the soft lamp of a moving face —
its own source
of surprised luminosity
a setting where one looks just

as one feels, firm
glowing like a glow worm

Because women make light
in a dark room (a fluid motion)
Because women reach
behind light with their bodies
adding warmth — a cup of sugar
making men feel their hair
this light situation
(office, home, morning light)
needs to be remedied
must be made truer
needs a great amount of shadow

FOR YOUR INFORMATION

free of pressing necessity and possessed
of considerable leisure, Count Leopardi,
an unspotted mammal of Italy,
poet and philologist, is dead

Leonid, on the other hand, appears overhead
once a year
on or about the fourteenth of November

there have been numerous Pope Leos
they were not heavenly bodies
anything pertaining to any of them is said to be Leonine
though there were thirteen
(there had been nine
at some point in history)

they appeared frequently on the Papal balcony
to toss blessings and dinner rolls to the crowds below
they had no discernible spots or manes

a mammal of Vinci, Leonardo,
invented many efficient war machines
and one irritating non-utilitarian smile
but no operas we know of
he was not an operatic composer
that was Leoncavallo
who galloped across life's pasture
and away, permanently,
leaving Pagliacci   then there's

Leonidas, King of Sparta, also extinguished
he died defending Thermopylae before Leonardo was born
before a lion raised his paw
and waved from a field of azure

the leopard is a loner, like Leonardo
but he's a ferocious carnivore
unlike da Vinci who didn't eat fish, beef,
lamb or poultry

nicknamed leopard lily, the spotted *lilium pardalinum*
of the western United States
reproduces freely

WHO'S TIRED

we brought you the Tired Rain
the Tiger's Paw
a Tire for the Rear reinforced
we brought you road bite

and the deep rub

side by side our tires go
even on wet roads, because we groove
straight, and today the pattern
is tireless traction

you want action

you want a tire
that wheels the car
you want to tread regular
in smooth mud

and contact

right off the bat
you want them tired hubs
side by side with more
rubber on the road

enraptured,

you'll put on a wide front
you'll get more tread rows
on our tires
you'll be so tired of tread rows
you'll yawn

which should ad up
(with extra mileage
and the deep lug)
to such rupture

you get out and push

adapted from Uniroyal Masters ad

BE A MAVERICK

do you want to be independent?
to have real passing power
to plug change, make points
and not be an orphan?

see your dealer

in a Maverick you go light
ride smooth, save gas,
spread your legs
they're designed that way

slip into a Maverick

if the headlamps grin
as your luggage slides from the roof
operate practically
skip plugs and points

forget about lube jobs

take the manual firmly in hand
crack a grill
kick a wheel, then
change dealers, midstream

THE RITZ

when your boat train from Calais
steams in with its smoke-faced

freight of men, fall in
the Ritz stays open

the night through our crew awaits
with a rich bouillabaisse

steered through our kitchen
you'll see your self

in every spotless pot
and gleaming cleaver   we care

so be prepared to lose
your heart   you won't depart

hungry we guarantee choice meats
the finest linen

our chef, who never naps,
keeps one eye peeled   he'll leap

agreeably to greet you
with rows of bone-white porcelain

that snap   we know your taste
feel free   fall in

with our impeccable tradition

EVERYONE KNOWS
WHAT HARTMANN IS ABOUT

you'll experience yourself
in two pieces   or as nineteen
different men and women
each piece vinyl

with the soft feel
of moccasin leather

the legendary heartmen —
with adjustable straps in men's
and women's sizes — belt you
you'll see striking colors

earth   clay   slate
take your choice

of necessity we're expensive
but — once a year —
to encourage you —
we make this compassionate offer

at a price
you can afford:

three strong grips
you'll beg for a fourth
once you experience heartman
you'll beg

adapted from an ad for Hartmann luggage

BIRDS EYE

inside every man
lives a little boy
who didn't like his vegetables
a little boy
who gave all the problems
to yesterday's mothers

but mothers never forget!

on a Saturday afternoon
the impossible happened
little Jimmy opened his mouth
and in went
the night, his mother,
swimming in onion sauce

adapted from Birds Eye ad

THE DIFFICULT COUNTRIES

lessons will get you no place
in waters churning with lavish hair
there are hardships
you won't find shiny floors
armies in attendance

you will shortly disappear
into the mouth of a gamefish
where the novelty
will cause you to worship —
hands clasped —
beyond the machinery
of verbal chic

you will not find bagels, chow
mein   you will not find beauty
furnished with a smooth disposition
in the difficult countries
you will be hunted by sun
prepared, by night,
for the final adventure

you won't meet anyone
on the promontories
of the snow-clad Andes
but as you slowly
turn and become a natural resource
you'll have the satisfaction
of knowing you arrived
before Conrad Hilton

adapted from an ad in The New Yorker

A SOMEONE AS GOOD AS ANY

a pantomime

onstage a large eye uncurtains
passengers board a train
someone runs down the aisle

leaps to the stage
kicks a hole in the scrim
. . . nothing in back

he implants an inhabited region
he waters it

posed nobly at its frontier
he accepts a fistful of daisies
without flinching

officials crack knuckles
and speak well of him

he ascends
he demonstrates
we applaud
he reverses direction and vibrates

he tilts the brim of his hat
lifts right trouser leg   unbuttons
shirt to expose hairless chest

a few boos   a pause

dealing eight fibs from the deck
he places them on the table
at right angles
his assistant applauds

he flaps his arms
barking loud significant sounds
we clap wildly

snatch his hat
rip his shirt from his back
yank out his eyes

he's floored

six hold him down
one slits his skin
another peers in   then

one by one . . .
sucked into the vacuum

IN THE SWIM

plunge, then strike out
kicking, swivelling the head, thrusting the arms

exhausting

so why strike out?

hunger
all motion begins with it

hunger to plug in, or be plugged into,
the juice of the universe
to get lit

curiousity? an exalted hunger, an appetite
of the cerebrum, the upper gut

once charged, the limbs themselves take over . . .
one hopes

chore or choreography; *which*
depends on your state of grace

or it's mating season

still, why budge   why not just . . .
sink
into that Sea of Selflessness
some so zealously pursue
with high-priced gurus

why pursue?   we do sink   every night

but I'm no ingrate   loyal to the hand
that casts me the rough rope at dawn,
I rise hang on get going

if you're no swimmer, travel light
rely on the current

one can progress and prosper
on currency alone

dollars for instance

one can get almost anywhere on a flood of them
and bring souvenirs home

"home" . . . to get back to it —
trip of a lifetime,
long and through foreign lands   take Ulysses. . . .

though home, after all, may be only
the empty gut we take with us

HOME

the family permits you to pack or it doesn't
you leave anyway with your particular diction
the crutch you move with was made for you

you think : even a poor man can dance
only the soldier, commanded, must stand firm

but now slip your arms in the hour's sleeves
and set out   vertical is the miracle
scissoring limbs cut seconds from unrolling time

at a stalk's summit, snails cluster
what did they hope to find?

you root a tower and climb it
toward love or power, suitcase filled with hats
bulbs and a pistol

gazing skyward you raise your arms, palms up
for stars   with stars one can buy anything —

even stars   and who can have enough of them
but stars run on their own batteries
they rush away

you have the right to protest . . .
later

in no-time — a painless defeat of space —

your mother inhabits your trunk
father fumbles for his glasses in the maze

where you disclose your whereabouts
to yourself by calling out

and home is the place you can't leave
the upholstered armchair you make
when you bend at the hips and the knees

INSCRIPTION FOUND ON A STELE CIRCA 1950

When the time came for the takeoff, I clung to the nest's rim. The drop was terrible; I felt it in my knees, my gut. Where was there to go after all. I was not a kite but an infant, not foolish enough for the simple falling out. So I hung on, barely able to shift my weight safely on the narrow ledge.

Winds found me and affected me keenly: seed-bearing winds, carrier winds transporting mosquito squadrons bound for blood. Gusts blew in and whisked away cousins on journeys to extinction.

My skin prickles when I consider those winds, though, to do them justice, they bore the rootless, the ill-treated, the restless, to wars in promised lands.

On clear days I'd squat where ledge met wall. I did not care to see the pebbles plummet. I had no wish to plunge, spread-armed, into the century. But I saw plenty. How could I help it at that altitude.

When thunderheads rolled in (those footholds for fantasy), I'd peek through gaps at the green and umber gameboard below. Jostling pinball-populations sped along mazes to a busyness in one hole or another. In solemn columns they rolled back to their starting points at evening.

Sites of wrecks drew me, those jackstraw castings, frozen histories of concussion from which rails, free of ties, curved upward in rainbow catenaries, more eloquent, in my opinion, than the Alhambra's cool geometries. I had books and a harrowing imagination if narrow means.

At times the earth rumbled as if to remind me of my origins, as if urging greater efforts to attain orbit, join wives, make sons.

It was not my fault, I shouted down, that a fluke of birth had deposited me close to the pinnacle.

I broadcasted this with my buttocks pressed to the granite wall, the same granite I now face, chisel between my teeth, one hand wedged in the crevice of my birth, one in a neighbor's fault, though just this morning a compassionate vulture, in passing, remarked that at my age the step down was a mere six feet and added, speaking of course from his experience, *anyone can fly.*

IN THE HALF LIGHT

Though highways don't remember my weight, I have travelled. I go where I can hide openly. My valise gets through duty-free.

Condensation on the panes makes it impossible to decipher street names. Rub with a glove and the glass streaks. Between blurred glass, large flakes falling beyond, and the angle of street signs, one feels quite lost.

Our driver, enclosed in a steel vault, occasionally responds to signals, but cannot be reached for questioning. Some discussion takes place among passengers straining to recognise landmarks. No one wants to be let off on a strange street with the mercury at zero.

Pre-dawn? late afternoon? The yellow-grey sky tells nothing. I don't know when I set out; for what destination.

At the next stop I descend behind a man clutching his hat who hurries, slipping and slanting into the snow. He may be headed for the same concert. I speed down the broad steps after him.

In the pink city the sun casts long shadows. Swimming through air, I enter a refectory where people practice instruments, each digesting his or her own music, an orchestral Last Supper. Unique chords and melodies harmonize like the droning of many bees. On the east wall the maestro, Christ, bleeds as though fed by an eternal spring.

Improvising, I begin to sing:

> Many come hungry to the grocery store
> Many go hungry because they came in poor
> But one doesn't ask, one doesn't buy

> This one takes what drops to the floor
> And no one asks the reason why

A white-haired gentleman looks up from his harp, annoyed.

Around me carriages bang. I too type frantically covering my paper with musical staff lines. In the turbulent wind sheets of paper scurry along race tracks to the ceiling, handicapped with information.

The horses stop and bend down long necks at the waterhole. Their backs conform to the silhouette of a distant mountain range. I tack up the sketch forcing myself to see, through the myopic fog, the horses' truth — that part of it, at least, that might illuminate my own exhausted leaps.

But now the mercury has dropped. Condensation on the panes makes it impossible to read the street signs. The driver, occasionally responding to signals, cannot be reached. I pull the cord and descend behind a man holding a small tuna. Is he also headed for the ocean?

The floor remains intact, hardly worn, where I've travelled from bed to window to table to bed to table.

FACTS

> "That which actually exists; reality; truth."
> — *Random House Dictionary*
>
> "Now, what I want is Facts. Teach these boys and girls nothing but Facts. Facts alone are wanted in life. Stick to the facts, sir!"
> — *Hard Times*, Dickens

We suspect facts are down to earth. We suggest they conduct business underground where there are no views, digging in at random. Crossing the yard after the morning news we find earthworks raised by their nocturnal armies, next to holes with no tenants. What is a "fact"? At night, at dawn, we lie in wait to face them. They elude us. Fences of course are over their heads. We can't trap them that way. We have developed minute electric beepers to attach to the first captives. We will track them, map their burrows. We Agnostics pursue them with vigor

Factions have sprung up; and factions within factions

The Spiritualists adopt the motto, "By their holes shall ye know them." The world is illusion, a lid thin as mist. Lift it and the pot is empty — except for Spirit. The steam that smacks you in the face is Spirit. Faith proves this a "fact" *a priori*. Spirit fills the pot with non-matter that propagates like yeast nourishing the void. They claim there is but one Spirit, with one face, a loving face, the face of the deep (though appearances, they agree, are deceptive) and one name. Only one sound intoned with sufficient vigor, and often, will summon the Spirit, the genie, who will effect a cure, a match, the displacement of a mountain that obscures one's view. About the name there is some dispute: Om, Jahweh, Allah, Ahura Mazda. ... The list is long. In the struggles of the agonists to reach consensus, many ectoplasmic limbs have been torn off, much ichor has poured from illusory ventricles

The materialists say, "Look to the mounds," . . . no need to look beyond them. The mounds inhabited the holes which remain mere topological irregularities. Matter, they say, *is* fact. No matter how pitted with holes, Matter may be grasped, kicked, ploughed, stored, capitalized. The more of it one accumulates, the more one matters. They call attention to the broad perspective achieved by mounting a pile, the Great Pyramids for instance — monuments to the fact of Matter and the matter of fact. Why else would humankind have crossed seas to ascend them, to stand gaping up at them. Burial under a pile guarantees immortality. Builders of piles have foundations named after them. Even in the form of walls, matters of fact impress. Try banging your head against one. Who can dispute the Great Wall of China

The Institute of Sceptics offers handsome rewards. Claimants arrive at headquarters by thousands hauling huge factories, flotillas, world systems. Highly trained specialists sit in judgement and pronounce them "guilty of point-of-view." Now and then an advocate pleads his cause with such dazzling conviction and pyrotechnic virtuosity that the judges are blinded by tears. Ever-watchful, believers rush in to envelop them in a firm fraternal embrace. They are transported. Their names are added to the list of defectors and hearings may be held up for decades

Unconcerned with microscopes and binoculars, with piles, walls and horizons, the Sensualists investigate all holes with their fingers, tongues and any other extension of themselves that will fit what they call "the living fact." They eschew discussion, preferring a mouthful of smoked whitefish. Though I look in on meetings of other factions, on my best days I am one of these

FROM THE BARRENS

To restock I take a stroll. I've left behind pencil and pad. I've no web or trap. Suddenly, without warning, genuine surfaces flood toward me like a field of wildflowers in a train window: faces, torsos, limbs — a rush-hour tide. I stagger in the face of the glittering mixed metaphors, entranced, but empty-handed

A few days ago, as I walked by the iron paling that separates the green skirt of the neighborhood Episcopal Church from the cement of Fifth Avenue, a rare phrase flashed and settled just out of reach among the crabapple blossoms. Yes, rare. *And* winged. (I have a nose for such things and I'm willing to be lifted, even carried away.) It took off, of course. I suspected a nest

Later I emptied my purse on the table and searched among the scattered vagaries. I found a few broken eggshells, yes, but with the color quite bleached away: "beauty" "truth" . . . nothing to stroke, to take hold of; no chick with the early plumage of its particular species. Nothing to incubate, or eat either. Nothing nourishing to me, to you, to anyone I know. Easter had come. And gone

Today I approached the churchyard again, murmuring to the inspired possible "Come, take me, take me!" There was the tree holding up a head heavy with prosaic foliage, but no bird, no blooms

A bit of life-yolk, brown, dry as old paste, clings to these shell shards. I stamp on them

THE SNEEZE, Notes for an Essay

A sneeze enlivens the air like a firecracker

But witness the happy perpetrator: folding suddenly as though shot in the belly, he sends his hand swiftly to his breast pocket. With cloth intervening, he grasps his nose and in a concerted effort his entire orchestra releases a tremendous fart-like gust against the nostrils. At this point the fingers open and shut like a clever valve, damming the sneeze midstream. Like the sound of a shofar announcing the New Year, this transforms the joyous explosion into a thunderous doom-filled prophesy, or several irate rapid blasts

Today the proud noun "sneeze" bears a weighty burden. Negative associations cling to it like aphids to a rose: itch, ache in the cheeks, continous leak, to name but a few deposited there, one suspects, by a cabal of allergists protecting their private interests. These are, mind you, great-grandsons of men and women who carried a precious powder in costly enameled boxes to clear their heads and provide instant delight during dull gatherings of a winter's eve

Surely such simple pleasure is of prime importance to a race dying of boredom

A sneeze is not a cough

Nature, in rare instances, overselects. In her exhuberance she goes out on a limb producing "sensitives" possessed, as it were, by a seasonal Dionysian madness

Is this Nature's warning to us to pursue pleasure in moderation? To quote Montaigne, "Let us permit nature to have her way: she understands her business better than we do"

We must consider the mainstream, the misled majority, who, rejecting their birthright, confine themselves in sealed rooms during the rose season, the season of ragweed, hay, and waggling golden tails. Needled by physicians, puritanical by education, they eschew the fresh spray of a sneeze, that cheerful human exflorescence

Fish do not sneeze

WHAT CAN BE THE USE OF THEM

Superficially they resemble each other like natives of a foreign land, guests, you might say, of our nation, who arrive without passports and stay without permits

We take them for granted

You might find them ursine, cool, slippery . . . perversely protean to the touch and, in that sense, exemplary conformists, but

unemployable,

manifestly, unredeemably unemployable. Too feeble by day to lift, clap, or press buttons, they'd bankrupt the state were they not so abstemious

they detest noon and shrink from it, collecting under bushes, benches and women's skirts

But early and late they stretch,

attach to anything upright and, running before or behind like court fools, mimic our slightest gestures

Under certain conditions they astound, amuse or terrify,

skimming walls with lizardlike agility, crouching, looming, leaping and shaking like inebriated shamans summoning our demons

Dusk finds them ravenous

They swallow everything in sight until at last, wholly shameless, they devour each other

As for their lovelife — lustful by nature, but instinctively shy, they hide till we put out the light, then slide from under our bedsteads

to embrace us entirely

BAD DAY

When the composer's cat caught his bird, it only did what it had not been taught not to do, so the composer couldn't, with justice, erect himself in his anger-pole, which anyhow no longer fit

Lowering his sad fat between the arms of a rocker that creaked mournfully, the composer mopped his steadily slipping face with a page of his sonata as he watched the bird's tail go down like a last childhood hop

The composer's infant lips made small waves as if shaping notes from a phrasebook in a strange country, a country without birds, where his cat peered from each tree quietly belching feathers

THE PROFESSOR

To E. H.

The Professor tilts his ponderous head as befits one who has been asked to address doctors, as one who has seen Greatness advance toward him waving a silk scarf from the back of her open Cadillac. He speaks with deliberation. A leaf of white hair slips down on his left temple as he releases a pun, a perfect cow pat

If slow of speech, the Professor is quick-eyed. Engrossed in twisting his goblet stem, turning water into wine, he spots a green lizard, high up, near the balcony swelling his pink throat out of season. He has no special use for the lizard, but graciously brings it to our attention. *His* attention is fixed on large prayers of the spirit

The Professor deliberates even while walking. But he misses nothing. In the course of his constitutional he notes fiddler crabs scuttling into holes by the hundreds. He has seen the heron. He has no time to stand still watching fiddler crabs, no patience with herons. He has somewhere to get to; somewhere to come back to. His spirit is very grand

Homeward bound, the Professor passes a lady peering through the long eyes of her binoculars. Quietly he slips behind a cabbage palm, then swiftly steps out, circling his eyes with his big fingers

She sees a dark hulk, a great animal. She gasps; looks again

"Why, it's the Professor!" she squeals. He's grinning like a found child. Enraptured she lowers her binoculars

No. Hands in his pockets, the Professor regards her ruefully, left ear inclined to his left shoulder

ASCENDING THE CAPE MEMLING'S MADONNA WEARS

the cape's steep slopes
are treacherous — vast
overhangs, ravines

rough threads grate his palms
yet

a haunting milk scent
permeates the air

from a fold's summit, he's seen
the Child's
bright buttock gleam

she shifts
the landscape quakes

sliding, he grips porous linen

will he attain the knee
to slip into those limbs,

to peer
through that wise
infant face?

held upright by her cool hands
free of clothes
and stress, He'll beam

and lean
to pinch the finger
of a kneeling queen,

bathed in Flemish clarity
close   the nipple
for Him alone

IN THE GAME FIND THE DOG

"where oh where has my little dog gone"

Y picks up the bill
and drops his coins on the table
each with a dog on one side
a profile on the other

this is the way it goes:

from across the field, the boy Y
sees a dot moving on the dirt road —
a dog?

there's someone with a sack
at the bottom of the sky

a car tears by
Y hears yelps from the road
the boy's eyes close on red
a red dragging shank

here come three men on bicycles
each with his rifle
yelling *which way d'he go?*
they confer at the blood-spill

from far away, Y — the man — shouts
put down those guns!
he'll get on with three legs

will they pick up the trail?

•

a waitress in blue lays change
in the dust   blood spoils the wine
there's salt in the breeze

oh earth   field   sky!

•

Y thinks he has seen a scar
on a moving mountain

in the game FIND THE DOG
was that him by the stream?

•

Y picks up his bill   puts coins
(dog-side up, or boy) on doodled plans:
rectangles, pierced circles
he has seen reason

he has seen
a grizzled dog by the cold stream
it slipped through the brush

Y goes on, limping

IT'S IN THE CARDS

a girl picks up the walls
of all her houses
and fans them in her hand

good deal! a rash of hearts
her strong suit
they itch under her skin

oh blushing season
the peacock spreads his tail
magnolias, their satin skirts

her hand slips
all the way in for a heart's
red bud

she arranges them in sequence

advancing
along the avenue lined with poplars
toward the great house

she picks a card:
wild strawberries
in the field behind the poplars,
or apples

her reach — longer than the arm —
collects them
to stack, stems down,
in pyramids

she passes

hearts burn out
turn black as spades
the poplars topple behind her

as she advances toward the gate
in the white wall, her eye
on the crest above it —

one heart,
sacred, still beating

THE PAINTER OF SKYSCAPES

the painter puts down his brush
loaded with blue
to consider the sky

clouds thoughtfully cast shadows

at one time a cloud
moody and purple as a sister
sat on him —

a crushing humidity

from a plump one hovering
a few large tears
descend on his meditations

he reaches up and squeezes

it plays Nut Brown Maiden
he opens his mouth
filling his soul with clouds

they rumble in his brain

as he penetrates cloudness
he vows not to weasel
out of anything planned for him

did not God appear to Job as a cloud?

understand cloudness and you grasp
the mechanics of heaven
yes, he has it!

he picks up his brush,

wipes it
loads it   presto!
a cow on the blue meadow

MANIPULATOR

a man has a stick, wool, marble
wrapping the stick in wool
he beats on the marble   no sound

draped in wool, he strides back and forth
on the marble with lifted staff
not one prophesy escapes his beard

he pitches the stick into a bush
kicks the wool
I've worked hard he thinks   *for what!*

his face drops into his hands
it bites off his thumbs
spitting them into the sky

wool sprouts from his pores
veins squirm through the marble
breaking it down so grass will spring up

and the stick?
oh the stick stands erect and roots
the old green tunes come back to it

baaa baaa calls the man-ram
baaa baaa the ewes answer
trotting to where he ruminates

in the shade of the stick-tree
flicking an ear
at the buzzing thumbs

MOON

weeping, a woman peels the moon
slices it
and drops it in the stew

a child spears the moon with a fork
it tastes like a pea —
mealy and sweet
many moons on her plate

a man cracks a moon
between legs of his compass
and eats the nut

the grand piano
carries a basket of pears and moons
on its polished mahogany back
one moon remembers the peck
of a cedar waxwing

Columbus loved her slow syllable
her scent of cinnamon and cloves

voyaging, always voyaging
she carries an orient
in her gleaming belly

now, behind torn veils, the moon
glows like a widow

THE OPTIMIST

jovial, I leap
the barricade   demons decamp
with my astrolabe

transplanted among cannibals
I eat platinum heroes   and words
to turn back the shade

lo how a day comes —
red tongue flapping — and trots away
parting the barley

I vault again — to pleasure
among yellow roses of Castille
sacred as the day's yolk

in my feather coat,
pecking under my nose,
I delete my debts

but wait! a clapper booms
the casket fills   it's my sister
the dough of her flesh rises

. . . must flap to a tree
look away from Señor Coyote
whirling below!

but when Death stuffs cracks
in my soles, I'll glow, bright
as a marigold

all night I affirm the sun
though it's small as an onion

DEFENDER OF THE FAITH

when I climb to parapets
of Eternal Law
and peer through binoculars
at our besiegers — dots
thick as anchovies
in the hostile sea
I think —

those could be our sons
squatting among the enemy
around seeds
stolen from our firetree
our sons
toasting their palms'
blank pages

they say swine
root at the base
of our Sacred Oak
and youths kiss
under a burning bush
hanged from sky's lintel
like red mistletoe

IN THE MIRACULOUS CHAPEL

for Russell Adams, artist
Taos, New Mexico

body drawn back, one eye shut,
you thrust an arm out — thumb up
to measure a mute absolute —
a domino dot on the night wall

a chair, a cross, a stiff crow
flow from your pen's beak
you want to fly
from the cool dry hole
in the chapel at Chimayo,

from crutches, canes, catching light
as they fall toward the healing pit
in your nest a phoenix smolders
light you shout   *it's the light!*

BEHIND SPRING'S RAISED FINGERS

she bids mirth,
the kind a skilled cook serves
palms to polish his surface
until the grain sings
a place to store trophies
hauled back from safaris
through creases in his cortex

and more:
when clouds drop low and their
paper plane naps on one wing,
she'll hook her purse of wild
schemes on a nail   let him fire
until the hidden spills

she bids reflections,
worth years, from her windshield
she's quit moving   upstairs,
under black cloth, the Boss
frames him for a passport
to her mirror room

she can't lose   his right
is her left hand's shadow

WORKING AT KNOTS

    wait, I say, for a package
    a rose

it came, she says
I worked at the knots, unwrapped a tin
painted with roses

    ah, I say

I lifted the lid, she says, and found
shattered cookies from mom

so I've a string — two feet
no striding out though

routes between tenants
twist and knot
to be picked at and reused in plots

we meet in the hall — smiles
luminous as needlefish

    but there are bridges, I say

in bed, she says
secure as a wallaby pouch —
a brief hush

but rise
and words race, out of touch

    well, I say, that's
    nothing to be accused of
    kiss the knots

DIALOGUE

SHE: what have you done to your voice
        it's a chill rain
        while you were gone I made a hoop
        for you   what did you dream?

HE: I dreamt my sack heaved and thrashed
        wisteria climbed my thighs
        I choked on the fat-sweet scent
        don't look now!   kiss me

SHE: then hand me a crystal to
        see where you've been, make me
        a rain saw, a stick for my hoop
        toss me your dream crutch

HE: crutch? I yanked and shoved
        the sack wouldn't budge
        how we'd chase under rain once
        I'd race through the thorn bush

SHE: squeeze closer
        whatever you've got there, I want one
        fix my motor so it sings
        listen, I've got to dash   hug me

HE: so dash   I'm cursed
        with this sack full of frogs
        ... and take your hope
        wait   roll me a kiss

FROM THE SOUK IN MARRAKESH

who are those passersby?
one holds a red ball
two walks a dog   three hides
under a green djelabba

there's a family likeness
in our shadows — leaves on a tree

moved by intriguing folds
to touch, I reach. . . .
there's the call to prayer!

give up the body's passage
for a life of mind?   not I

while you search history's page
a cobra lifts its head, I rise
the shutter snaps

draped on lines between roofs,
skeins, dyed red and yellow, dry

that passerby?   that's me,
disguised, under sky's
searing blue — one banner
over our strangeness

About the Author

Carolyn Stoloff is a poet and a painter. Her previous volumes of verse include *Stepping Out* (Unicorn Press), *Dying to Survive* (Doubleday & Co.), *Swiftly Now* (Ohio University Press), and *A Spool of Blue, New and Selected Poems* (Scarecrow Press). Over the past twenty years Ms. Stoloff has published her poems in such magazines as *The New Yorker, The Nation, Partisan Review, Kayak, Chelsea* and *Caliban*. Her work has also been anthologized in *Rising Tides, Alcatrez, Asylum Annual, New Directions*, and *The New Yorker Book of Poems*. She has received grants for her poetry from the National Council on the Arts, the MacDowell Colony and other foundations. She is a long-time resident of New York City.